T0124220

OFF-THE-TOP TREASURES

JAY WILLIS

OFF-THE-TOP TREASURES

iUniverse books may be ordered through booksellers or by contacting:

iUniverse
1663 Liberty Drive
Bloomington, IN 47403
www.iuniverse.com
1-800-Authors (1-800-288-4677)

Because of the dynamic nature of the Internet, any web addresses or links contained in this book may have changed since publication and may no longer be valid. The views expressed in this work are solely those of the author and do not necessarily reflect the views of the publisher, and the publisher hereby disclaims any responsibility for them.

Any people depicted in stock imagery provided by Getty Images are models, and such images are being used for illustrative purposes only. Certain stock imagery © Getty Images.

ISBN: 978-1-5320-9453-8 (sc)
ISBN: 978-1-5320-9454-5 (e)

Library of Congress Control Number: 2020902480

Print information available on the last page.

iUniverse rev. date: 02/10/2020

DEDICATION

I write this collection of sayings for all my relatives, wherever they may exist. They are scattered from Maine to California and from Mexico to Alaska.

ACKNOWLEDGMENT

Thanks to my brother Wade
for being a true Guardian Angel.

CONTENTS

PREFACE

This collection of sayings came from several different sources: my background, experiences, and creative conscious. Most of them came from my creative conscious. Some of them are common sayings that I have memorized from hearing others repeat over and over throughout my lifetime. None of them were deliberately taken from another written source. If any of them came from another written source I am not aware of it. They didn't come from another book, or any familiar source, but most of them came from the deep recesses of my mind. I did use a few of the more commonly used sayings. Some of these sayings are simply passed on through the grapevine. It would take a lifetime of research to trace some of these folk sayings to their original source.

I started with sayings, and ended up including some of my personal and private thoughts. I conceived these thoughts and sayings while sitting in my La-Z-Boy, in front of the fireplace, with a warm-comfortable blanket.

Occasionally, I meditated at the local library. I wrote these sayings during the long, extremely cold winter of 2018-19.

To write these sayings I used a process I call stream-of-consciousness brainstorming, where I simply wrote what came to mind, after forcing my mind to engage.

I have entitled this collection of sayings, *Off-the-Top Treasures: A Collection of Sayings*, because they are mostly a product of my own cerebral creations. Anyone can go to another source and select sayings for his own use.

I decided to stretch my wings, and to go for what I knew. These sayings reflect my thoughts about some important issues. It is the way in which I see the world. They present my thoughts on getting along and surviving in a world of dung.

My writing is like what my parents felt about parenting, "let the hair go with the hide." Meaning: let children be what they will be. "They will usually find their way." In this way my writing speaks for itself, and it can be whatever the reader wants it to be.

These sayings are not erudite, but are plain and simple—yet, profound and thought provoking. They contain wisdom I developed over the years.

Some people are already aware of what these sayings imply. I only give them as food for thought, something for the reader to re-think. I quoted one of my sayings to another individual once. The person said, "Everybody knows that already." I don't believe most people are already cognizant of most of these sayings. Some of these sayings may not have any meaning for some, but most will find them meaningful.

People often ask me why I write. I tells them I write because when I am writing I am in my comfort zone. I feel a need to express what's on my mind, and to tell my truths.

I hope this collection of sayings will be stimulating, inspiring, and thought provoking. Check out this collection and other of my books @ jaythomaswillis.com or buybooksontheweb.com or amazon.com.

Jay Thomas Willis
Richton Park, Illinois

ABOUT THE AUTHOR

J AY THOMAS WILLIS is a graduate of the University of Houston, Houston, Texas, where he earned a Masters' degree in social work; he is also a graduate of the Masters' degree counselling program at Texas Southern University, Houston, Texas. He attended undergraduate school at Stephen F. Austin State University, Nacogdoches, Texas, where he earned a B.S. degree in sociology and social and rehabilitative services.

He worked as a Clinical Social Worker for seventeen years, providing direct clinical services as well as supervision. He has been a consultant to a nursing home and a boys' group home; taught college courses in sociology, family, and social work in community college and university settings; and has worked as a family therapist for several agencies in the Chicago area. In addition, he was a consultant to a number of home-health care agencies in the south suburbs and Chicago. Mr. Willis is a past CHAMPUS peer reviewer for the

American Psychological Association and the American Psychiatric Association. He also spent a number of years in private practice as a Licensed Clinical Social Worker in the State of Illinois.

Mr. Willis has traveled and lectured extensively on the condition of the African American community. He has written thirty-three books, and written many journal articles on the subject of the African American community. He has written several magazine articles. He has also written Op-Ed Commentaries for the *Chicago Defender, Final Call, East Side Daily News* of Cleveland, and *Dallas Examiner*. He currently lives in Richton Park, Illinois with his wife and son.

ALSO BY JAY THOMAS WILLIS

Nonfiction

A Penny for Your Thoughts: Insights, Perceptions, and Reflections on the African American Condition

Implications for Effective Psychotherapy with African Americans

Freeing the African-American's Mind

God or Barbarian: The Myth of a Messiah Who Will Return to Liberate Us

Finding Your Own African-Centered Rhythm

When the Village Idiot Get Started

Nowhere to Run or Hide

Why Blacks Behave as They Do: The Conditioning Process from Generation to Generation

God, or Balance in the Universe

Over the Celestial Wireless

CHAPTER 1

On Spirituality and Religion

"Hell is when you are out of balance with the universe; Heaven is when you are in right-balance."

"Sometimes, you've got to storm the gates of hell, and take what belongs to you."

"Hell is not down below, and Heaven is not in the sky; we experience Heaven and hell on a daily basis."

"The Almighty God comes back for someone every day. This God is not going to soon return on a silver cloud, in a blaze of glory, and take you to a home in the sky."

"The only chariot you are going to ride out of here on is that long-black hearse."

"The Almighty God has a unique plan
for each and every one of us."

"It may seem as though you can't make it,
but keep making an effort, the Almighty
God has a definite plan for you."

"Don't let anyone convince you that you are not
the highest creation of God's imagination."

"When we learn to respect and love our
brothers and ourselves, we will be closer
to achieving our so-called salvation."

"There is a little of God within each of us. Don't focus
on the sky, Heaven, the clouds, and other places."

"After many years, some people are still threatened
by talk against the slave master's religion."

"When you look at a tree, inhale, or see a baby
born, you know the Almighty God exists."

"If you are given a book, and told it contains the
Word of God. Sent to church every Sunday and
reinforced with the idea that God is alive—every day.
Soon you will come to believe in this God, whether
he is real, or only a figment of your imagination."

"Go to church. The church has some good values. I have heard that people who attend church regularly are less likely to go to prison, more likely to graduate high school, go to college, and more likely to succeed in life."

"After praying to every God you know without results; try balance, justice, harmony, order, truth, righteousness, and reciprocity."

"We need more justice, balance, order, harmony, reciprocity, righteousness, and truth, than we need more of religion."

"Don't wait for divine intervention; get off your behind, and help yourself."

"You can't get away with anything; because, there is justice and balance in the universe."

"Work hard, party hard, and laugh hard; for you never know when the Almighty God is coming for you."

"We search for God in all the wrong places; yet, we fail to look inside ourselves."

"We depend on something unreal to give us power in our daily lives."

"There is not one credible shred of evidence that any of the characters in the Bible ever existed."

"The fear of the Almighty God should eliminate all prejudice, discrimination, bigotry, and racism."

"No one has ever or will ever carry your burden for you. It might give you comfort to think so. But you must carry your own so-called burden."

"Nobody can help you to know the Almighty God; you got to get to know Him for yourself."

"Let the spirit within you speak to you, guide you, and teach you."

"Spirituality and the Almighty God will sustain you during times of hardship."

"Spirituality is important for our growth and development."

"The Savior is not coming, the Savior is here, that Savior could possibly be you."

"The Almighty God intended for you to be happy and prosperous in your existence."

"You weren't an accident; the Almighty God designed and placed you in this particular place, space, and time for a reason; you should make the most of it."

"The Almighty God will take care
of you for His own glory."

"No! the Lord is not going to make a way
or provide for you; unless, you get off
your behind and make an effort."

"The Almighty God has prepared you
to handle your adversities."

"Religion is a lie that sometimes
produces favorable results."

"Don't throw your belief in an Almighty God
out with your belief in a religious lie."

"Some people don't have the slightest idea about
who or what God is, other than that God given
to us by Western religion and the Bible."

"Some people like to make deals with God when
they get under pressure. But the Almighty God
is not in the business of making deals."

"Everything in my experiences tell me
that the Almighty God is in control."

"When you believe in something unreal,
don't expect real results."

"Ministers say, 'all you've got to do is believe'; but some people believe and do the best they can all their lives, and never seem to reap any blessings or benefits."

"There is no Heaven and no hell, only six-feet under, or conversion to ashes. Our death is the end of our existence."

"Nobody is greater than thyself but the Creator Himself."

"The Almighty God knew what He was doing when He made you. If He had wanted to make somebody else, He wouldn't have made you."

"Being in ministry means giving of yourself when those you are giving to may or may not appreciate it."

"In ministry you love people; even though they may try to hurt you."

"The Almighty God is not interested in you being anyone else, or who you could have been, only in you being who He made you to be."

"Deliver yourself: and live the life that the Almighty God has purposed for you to live."

"No matter how much you go to church and claim Jesus as your Savior; pray, praise, tithe, and worship; you are still going to have to pay for your transgressions."

"Nobody is going to bear your burden, and nobody has paid for your so-called sins."

"There will be no rapture, and Jesus is not coming back."

"You can't claim to be saved, and expect that you are forgiven for all your negative behavior. You must live a balanced, wholesome, and righteous life in order to attain what is referred to as salvation."

"When you stumble and fall, the Almighty God will pick you up."

"There is no life after death."

"It is difficult to take away from an individual what the Almighty God has given him or her."

"God knew what He was doing when He made you. God doesn't make mistakes, and He doesn't make junk."

"Demand balance, justice, order, truth, harmony, righteousness, and reciprocity wherever you go."

"The Bible may not be real or historical, but within it there is something to be learned."

"Evidence outweighs faith: when you have evidence, you don't need faith."

"Don't transform metaphysical statements into reality."

"Live your life so as to experience Heaven now rather than waiting to get to a place beyond the skies."

"Instead of appealing to God to help yourself or someone else, why don't you make an effort."

"Justice on earth shouldn't require the consideration of a Heaven or hell."

"When we get too caught up on going to Heaven, we sometimes lose our earthly value."

"In looking towards the Heavens, we lose our perspective on our individual potential."

"If we believe in each other, we can find meaning in life."

"If you believe in something, and actually work toward it, it'll work out for you."

"We have an obligation to create a humane society, and to make life better for each other, regardless of our religion."

"Always demonstrate goodness, righteousness, and compassion in your relationships."

"One can be religious and be a rogue of veritable background."

"Religion has done us some good, but it has also kept us from making wholesale progress."

"We are powerless to know absolutely about the existence of God."

"The finite cannot understand the infinite."

"If you have balance, truth, order, reciprocity, harmony, justice, and righteousness in your life; you don't have to worry about your soul."

"Heaven and hell are religious concepts thought up by men just like you and me."

"There is balance and justice in the universe. 'What goes up must come down.' 'What goes around comes around.' 'For every action there is an equal and opposite reaction.' 'If you dance to the music you must pay to the piper.' And there's nothing anyone can do about it."

"You can't destroy harmony, justice, and balance in the universe; you can disrupt them in some aspect, but they will continue to flourish."

"It is true that you can't beat the house when playing at a casino; you also can't beat the balance and justice in the universe."

"The only reason why you're still here is because the Almighty God intended for you to survive."

"Everyone might have their plans for you, but the Almighty God has the final say."

"You might feel bad about yourself momentarily, but remember you are beautifully and wonderfully made by the Almighty God."

"Don't get your priorities confused, and remember the Almighty God is still in control."

"You can't get away with craftiness, murder, mayhem, deceit, and treachery; the Almighty God will hold you accountable, one way or the other."

"Your payback for your transgressions may not come back to you when you expect it, how you expect it, but it will ultimately come, everyone has to pay for their transgressions."

"If you are blessed enough to go through fire without getting burned, maybe the Almighty God is trying to tell you something."

"The quickest way to hell is through mistreating others."

"Treat yourself and all others with dignity and respect; these are some of the keys to your salvation."

"It's not my duty to repay my enemies for their negative and destructive behavior; it's up to the Almighty God."

"You will be held accountable for all the destruction and havoc you create in other people's lives."

"The only way out of our predicament is righteous living."

"Respect, peace, joy, and love for our fellow man will also be our salvation."

"The moral arc of the universe bends toward justice, balance, order, truth, harmony, righteousness, and reciprocity, etc."

"We need more science, skill, and technology in our community; more than we need religion."

"It's necessary to replace the joy of the lie with the pain of the truth."

"Some people will misuse you, hide behind religion, and claim to be saved."

"Some people will try to stop you from becoming what the Almighty God intended for you to be. It's like stopping a caterpillar from becoming a butterfly or the tadpole from becoming a frog."

"Some people spend today worried about an afterlife. But you shouldn't destroy today worried about what will happen when you die."

CHAPTER 2

On Limitations

"You can't make a silk purse out of a sow's ear."

"Conflict is good, but if you have hard and long
destructive battles with anyone, you need
to limit your interactions with them."

"If you realize you are being mistreated, don't suffer
the consequences, figure out how you can move on."

"Knowing one's limitations is a special
gift and quality; whether it concerns your
strengths or your weaknesses."

"Don't let anyone push you beyond your
limits. Know when it's time to say no."

"A bird can't fly if its wings are clipped."

"The road less traveled may have
its own special limitations."

"For your own physical and emotional
health, realize your limitations."

"Be responsible for yourself; you can have only
limited responsibility for anyone else."

"Everybody has limitations: be sure you recognize
your strengths and your weaknesses. Know
when you are approaching your limits."

"The oppressor has never; in any place, space, or time,
told the oppressed something for their own good."

"If you don't broaden your horizon, you won't know
what your limitations are, or what your potential is."

"The only reason why you're in the position you're
in is because of the choices you've made."

"Life is nasty, brutal, and short; then we die."

"You can break one fragile stick, but many of these
sticks tied together are not easily broken."

CHAPTER 3

On Well Being

"An eagle makes the nest uncomfortable when it's time for her babies to vacate the nest."

"A hen will only scratch for her chicks until they can scratch for themselves."

"If you condition a person severely and consistently it will be a long time before that conditioning becomes extinct."

"Be kind to all; because, you never know who's going to be there when you fall."

"If you can't make it one way, try something different, you always have an alternative."

"Slow it down, take your time, what
God has for you is for you."

"Sometimes when you go to your brother or sister
for help they will knock you to your knees."

"The main ones you push aside may be the
only ones there in difficult times."

"If you should find yourself in a hole with a
shovel, don't start digging, trying to escape."

"Your undisciplined mind is your biggest problem."

"Take time to smell the roses in spring, the coffee in
the morning, and feel the rays of the midday sun."

"Don't let anyone tell you what is best for you."

"Don't ever quit, give up, give in,
surrender, or punk out."

"Stay alert, stay focused, and stay prepared."

"Time has moved on. Don't keep
focusing on the same old issues."

"If you think we live in a post-racial society, be
at the wrong place at the wrong time."

"You can't say certain things, because if you accuse someone without complete supportive details, they're going to say you're paranoid."

"The person is more important than the point."

"Don't run after the opposite sex, develop you character, so the opposite sex runs after you."

"Develop your courage, your faith, your purpose, and your dignity; and move forward."

"It does no good to be good at impression management but inadequate otherwise. People will see through you."

"If your love one abandons you, love the one you're with."

"Never raise a point which you cannot defend. Some points are indefensible."

"Your morals are the most important thing that you possess, don't compromise on them."

"The only thing important is at the end of life, be able to say, I had a good run for my money."

"It's hard for a behavior to become extinct when you are being reinforced on a daily basis."

"Don't believe everything people tell you;
research the validity for yourself."

"Don't try to convince a person to change their
beliefs; let him arrive at his own conclusions."

"It's a strenuous search, but don't quit
searching until you find your passion."

"As long as we're disrespecting, killing,
maiming, and fighting each other, we can
never as a people sustain ourselves."

"Hang on to the world, as it spends around.
Don't, let it get you down. Take it from
me, someday we'll all be free."

"We must learn to develop critical thinking
skills; some of us consider it a sin to think."

"Be careful about letting your opinions
become your convictions."

"Everyone believes their own views
are the correct way to think."

"All you've got to do to improve your situation
is to connect the dots, put two and two
together, and use your intelligence."

"Quit sabotaging yourself by deciding at the beginning
that a new situation is not going to work."

"People fail because they choose a state
of life and refuse to change."

"Learn the necessity of the development of
your personal sense of empowerment."

"Those things that are a hindrance to your
development are dysfunctional to your existence."

"As a result of being afraid of tomorrows
sorrows, we destroy today."

"There comes a time when you must roam again,
and renew your search for peace of mind."

"You can't make anyone happy, if the person
does not have the inner resources to be happy,
he or she will forever be unhappy."

"Sometimes it becomes necessary to say, 'I
am living the rest of my life for me.'"

"Life is a continuous search for peace of mind."

"When you think you have come to the end of
your patience, do some soul searching."

"We all have similar needs: we get hungry, we
need sleep, and we seek freedom from pain."

"Finances cause more problems in relationships
than any other single factor."

"We will all encounter difficulties in our lives.
We must strive to make the best of them."

"Respect other people's wishes and ideas."

"It's easy to let the pressures of life drive you to drink,
use drugs, gamble, or other inappropriate behaviors."

"You being a good person will last in the
hearts and minds of other people."

"Life is difficult enough; don't go chasing down yellow-
brick roads, looking for waterfalls, and pots of gold."

"Don't let you mouth get engaged before
your brain has a chance to."

"Don't let a thought take aim, bury itself
inside your brain, and refuse to leave. Get
rid of those obsessive thoughts."

"Don't wait until your partner becomes self- and other-
destructive before you decide it's time to move on."

"It's good to be comfortable expressing
yourself. If you can't express yourself, you
will be forever behind the eight ball."

"Sometimes we must create something
out of a deep void of nothingness."

"If we start out behind the eight ball, we will forever be
in this position—unless we improve our conscious level."

"Don't be guilty of being a party to helping to create
the conditions for your own destruction and demise."

"The best way to not come to a bad end is not to get
involved in the negative situation in the first place."

"If you fall in love, try not to fall so hard, you
don't want to make a fool of yourself."

"Don't engage in any behavior that is stupid, illegal, or
otherwise inappropriate. Maintain your reputation."

"When we fixate on people not liking us it's
usually because we have some serious issues."

"If you pay undue attention to what everyone says
and does, you are not going to get very far."

"Invest in other people, but don't lose
yourself in that investment."

"It will be to your advantage to build a
brick house on a cement foundation."

"You can go back home, providing you have
transportation, but things will not likely be
the same as when you left years ago."

"If people make demands on you that your
background can't accommodate, at least make
an effort, it will lead you to a greater destiny."

"If your friends front you off, triangulate you, and turn
their back on you; you need to make new friends."

"Be leery of those offering something
substantial for practically nothing."

"Everybody needs somebody, and if we live long
enough, we will need somebody to lean on."

"If you behave in a negative manner you will
probably get a negative consequence."

"Sometimes the medicine is responsible
for the negative condition."

"Negative conditioning in society will
produce negative behaviors."

"Never eat what your enemy brings to you on a plate."

"We are often attracted to things that
we are diametrically opposed to."

"We all seek love, attention, and affection. We must
have these things in order to be emotionally secure."

"Don't hang around with people who
have many obvious hangups."

"Sex is a huge rage, and many find it irresistible,
but best experienced in the context of a
marital relationship—not for recreation."

"So, you've had some difficult times in your life; make
a new start, and look forward to a brighter future."

"Sometimes you think you are absolutely
messed up and a total loss; but pick yourself
up, dust yourself off, and get back in the
game. You must see yourself as a winner."

"Nobody ever quit on an activity and at the
same time was successful at the activity."

"You may be experiencing difficulty, but
you've come too far to abandon your
dreams. Re-evaluate, and start again."

"A lifetime of degradation, humiliation, maltreatment, and other abuses will cause you to likely have some post-traumatic stress."

"If we think and speak positively, we will create positive energy in our lives; if we think and speak negatively, we will create negative energy in our lives."

"When you are in a stressful situation, your body will speak to you."

"Psychological stresses over a period of time will likely cause you to have some physical problems; and physical problems over a period of time will likelycause you to have some psychological stresses."

"Be sure you don't sabotage yourself when faced with a crucial opportunity."

"Don't lose sight of your humanity; see each individual with potential to be realized. Each individual should be able to maximize in this potential."

"We can't get to where we want to go until we can help others along the way."

"Nothing bad is going to happen if you return to the awareness of yourself."

"Always represent your family, school, church, community, and other organizations with which you are involved; put your best foot forward."

"Don't spend your life chasing cheap thrills, fine clothes, top-of-the-line cars, and expensive whiskey."

"The road to hell is paved with good intentions, but often fail to get us to our destination."

"Don't listen to all the negative talk, take control, and forge ahead."

"You can look all you want, but don't violate anyone else's space with your hands."

"If your enemy tells you something is no good, maybe you should give it a try; if he tells you something is good for you, leave it alone. Your enemy is not going to give you positive advice."

"Don't listen to anyone who has proven that they don't have your best interest at heart."

"Getting it together is a process rather than a state of being; at any one place, space, or time."

"You didn't come this far to give up now. Dust yourself off, and get back in the game."

"If not before, you will definitely have
it all together when you die."

"Don't get involved and play games with
self- and other-destructive people."

"Don't cry wolf so many times that nobody
believes you when the real threat comes."

"Don't associate with self- and other-destructive
people, you might lose your perspective, and
become something you're not supposed to be."

"We need good role models, but be careful
who you attempt to imitate. If you imitate
a fool you are going to become a fool."

"If you let yourself get involved in the game, you
better realize that you've got to pay to play."

"When we get involved in a deceitful game, many
times it doesn't turn out the way we planned."

"Don't be so concerned about getting yours;
if you help others you will get yours."

"If you don't believe in yourself nobody
else will believe in you."

"Without self-confidence you are nothing."

"Some people are messed up from the floor up, but want you to believe they have it all together."

"You knew what that particular activity would lead to; what did you think was going to happen?"

"If you don't have respect for yourself you won't have respect for anyone else."

"Don't let your initial conditioning control you for the rest of your life. Develop your conscious level, and find a way to rid yourself of this conditioning."

"Your conditioning will continue to influence you; unless, you can find a way to make it become extinct."

"Never let anyone else see you, and don't see yourself as a victim."

"A big house, fine clothes, and expensive cars alone won't make you happy. And poverty won't make you happy either."

"The solution to our insecurity is to seek and obtain peace of mind."

"Play, party, laugh, be happy; for death will come like a thief in the night, and steal your joy."

"Too many of us feel we have plenty of
time to accomplish our objectives in life,
and many of us run out of time."

"Don't get caught up in the black widow syndrome."

"Take good care of yourself; no one
is going to do it but you."

"Your negative attitude is part of your problem."

"Some people don't have a snowball's chance in
hell of surviving the social, economic, political,
educational, and psychological gravity in society."

"You saw it coming, you knew something was wrong
about that situation, yet you let it develop."

"You are not a sitting duck; you can't afford
to just let people take pot-shots at you."

"Nature is wonderful; isn't it strange how an ugly
caterpillar becomes a beautiful butterfly."

"You must rid yourself of your self- and other-destructive thoughts. It's the only way you are going to survive."

"Learn to profit from other people's mistakes, rather than make your own, and thus subjecting yourself to a process of trial and error."

CHAPTER 4

On Aggression

"In the end you must determine your own destiny."

"The only way to get ahead and stay ahead is through maximum and consistent effort and hard work."

"Always go the limit in working at attaining your objectives."

"Keep your head toward the sky, your nose against the grindstone, and your mind on a better tomorrow."

"Be vigilant; don't let any grass grow under your feet."

"Give it everything you've got, and then some, but don't keep butting your head against the wall."

"Sometimes running gets us there too fast,
and we need to take a slow-even pace."

"Go after your heart's desire; regardless
of the perceived obstacles. In the end
you will feel better about yourself."

"Nobody ever lost anything by simply putting forth
a concerted effort and have much to gain."

"Get off your behind and make a move, even if it's
the wrong move, it's better than just sitting there."

"You have all the keys you need to open the lock of
life; all you have to do is insert and turn the key."

"Don't be a fragile vessel waiting to crack;
get up and handle your situation."

"Always have a plan 'A,' a plan 'B,' and a
plan 'C'; because the best laid plans of mice
and men do sometimes go awry."

"Quit looking for an easy path from point 'A' to 'B,'
and learn to forge a path through rough terrain."

"When considering a serious negotiation,
always bring something to the table."

"We need to disconnect ourselves from that
which keeps us from being liberated."

"Nobody can change your situation but you."

"Don't get overly aggressive: there's room at
the table for all of us. The Almighty God has
provided all the necessary resources."

"Don't worry if people laugh at you. Be big,
bold, bad, and bodacious. Jump right in the
middle of the action without hesitation."

"The greatest military officer is the one who can take
control of the land without spilling any blood."

"Quit running, slow down, you have all the time
in the world to accomplish your objectives."

"You can ignore the reality all you want, but it's hard
to miss a freight train barreling down on you."

"Avoid people when they show signs of
being self- and other-destructive."

"Don't sell out, take a stand, and never give
up on accomplishing your objectives."

"Your future looks much better than your situation
looks right now. Keep working at it, and don't give up."

"Don't lose focus, don't drift, and don't become distracted from your objectives."

"There comes a time when you have to make that move—right now."

"Play the game well or don't play at all."

"If people have their doubts about you, don't let it get the best of you. Keep putting forth effort."

"If life has gotten you down, figure out a way to come back swinging. It's not over."

"Slow down, take your time, relax; if you are nervous and anxious you are going to lose control and fumble the ball; you will get what God has for you."

"There's no such thing as trying too hard. Give it everything you've got and then some."

"God will provide: if you are aggressive at pursuing what you want. God helps those who help themselves."

"God provides for those who are willing to help themselves."

"Times have changed, we must make the necessary changes to accommodate them."

"The worst possible thing you could do is give
up, and see yourself as a loser and a failure."

"Hold on! don't be so quick to give up.
You're a fighter, not a quitter."

"In life times will get tough, but you
must always take a stand."

"When you have everything against you,
simply jump in with both feet."

"Sometimes you have no alternative
but to go for what you know."

"If you keep pursuing, doing the best you
can, you will come out ahead."

"When your back is against the wall, show
your enemy what you are made of."

"The world is not coming to an end; unless, some
fool country releases a powerful bomb. Plato in 300
BCE thought the world was coming to an end."

"We are not sheep headed to the slaughter;
we can control our own destiny."

"You are worthy and capable of great accomplishments.
All you have to do is be persistent at making an effort."

"Don't wait for divine intervention: get
off your high horse and get busy."

"Don't just lie there in your bed: get
up and find something to kill."

"Achievement is directly proportional
to the amount of effort."

"If you find your natural element, and get
busy, you can easily reach your potential."

"When you find yourself running wild, slow it
down, and re-evaluate your priorities."

"You've got to make a tremendous effort if
you want to get out of your situation."

"Sometimes you've got to jump in with both feet;
even though you are nervous and unsure of yourself."

"Be big, bad, bold, and bodacious;
don't let anything deter you."

"So, what if you are out of your class, and out of your
league, act as if whatever it is belongs to you."

"You can accomplish your objectives. Don't
let anyone keep you from destiny."

"Nobody is going to solve your problems for you."

"Quit expecting someone else to make the necessary changes in society. Get up and do something yourself."

"Most people will encounter many obstacles in their lives, but should let nothing stop them from achieving their objectives."

"You need to stop the procrastination, and get up and make a vigorous effort."

"Fantasies are not destructive as long as you don't act on them."

CHAPTER 5

On the Universe

"It is balance, justice, order, truth,
harmony, righteousness, and reciprocity
that controls the universe."

"There is an abundance of resources in the universe;
take your time and get what belongs to you."

"When you get in balance with the universe, the
Almighty God will answer your prayers."

"We live in a universe that is sometimes nasty,
brutal, and short; don't let it keep you from
moving forward, while getting the best of you."

"Hell is not down below; but in the social, psychological, political, economic, and educational forces that exist in the universe."

"Everything should be done in moderation. Too much of anything is not good for you. The universe functions from a balanced perspective."

"Live your life in coordination with the universe. Don't try to control nature."

"It is necessary to be in harmony with nature, not against nature."

"The nature of the universe dictates that we will all one day get it together."

"To live in peace and harmony with the universe, you need to learn to listen to your inner voice."

"Nobody can escape the pendulum syndrome. The ups and downs of life are inherent in the universe."

"The ups and downs of the universe, the obstacles and adversities in life, grinds us down, but also polishes us up."

"Energy reverberates throughout the universe. And whatever energy we send out it comes back to us."

CHAPTER 6

On Assessing Your Situation

"Most of us have the similar fears, shed
similar tears, and die in so many years."

"Most of us are similar and respond in similar
ways: if you puncture us, we will bleed; if
you push us off balance, we will fall; and
if you attack us, we will retaliate."

"Some people don't like you because
they want to be you."

"If you can't work it out today,
tomorrow is another day."

"You can't get to where you want to go unless
you make some changes in your life."

"If you don't know which way to go, look in the mirror, and take a good look at yourself."

"If you don't have any plans for yourself, chances are you're not going anywhere."

"Sometimes we move too fast for our own good."

"Always take three steps ahead, because people will push you back two steps, in that way you will always be one step ahead."

"If you have to get to the top by deception, craftiness, and deceit; it's not worth it, you will dislike who you have become."

"If you feel you will hate yourself in the morning, don't go through with it tonight."

"Don't let your feelings and your emotions get in the way of your good judgment."

"What you feel, what you wish, and what you hope is irrelevant to what is real."

"Some people have more material things than you, but that's only a superficial advantage. Nobody has absolute advantage."

"Everybody has an angle, be sure you know yours,
and that of your friends and associates."

"If you didn't come from a comfortable place, fortify
your strengths, and develop your weaknesses."

"Sometimes those who have every possible
material thing are no more comfortable with
themselves than those who are penniless."

"Without purpose we are only fumbling
and groping in the darkness."

"People will get on your case, but don't let
them keep you from your destiny."

"Sometimes, it seems that you can't make progress,
but go for what you know, keep getting up."

"The only thing keeping you from your
goal is you undisciplined mind."

"Half of you task is just getting up."

"Don't cooperate with your own
destruction and demise."

"The right time to work on achieving
your goals is right now."

"Always make the supreme effort."

"Defy all those who would set up
stumbling blocks in your way."

"Sometimes, you have to find a quiet place
and meditate, although it is not good
to spend too much time alone."

"Take time to make time for your own
enrichment and development."

"They say you can't make it in this world
alone, but you don't need someone who's
carrying too much excess baggage."

"It's sometimes hard to walk away, but
realize when it's time to move on."

"You need to sometimes be around people who are
going to give you an honest opinion of yourself, and
not those who are going to always stroke your ego."

"The sky is not going to fall if you take
time to be kind to someone."

"Be kind to everyone, but don't let them
take your kindness for a weakness."

"Don't let your past conditioning lead you around like leading a horse to a spring."

"If someone smiles in your face one minute, and tries to stab you in your back the next; don't play that game, stay away from them."

"Don't be quick to judge, but don't let anyone pull the wool over your eyes."

"After you do everything you can to get along, and it still doesn't work, make a deliberate move."

"People come into your life for a reason, a season, or a lifetime; sometimes people are not meant to stay together, know when it's time to move on."

"Be careful when you allow people to come into your life; some people are too self- and other-destructive."

"Sometimes the solution to a problem is staring you right in the face, and you just haven't considered what is apparent."

"The right thing to do is the only thing to do."

"The only good reason to give up is because you are positive you have exhausted all other options, efforts, and alternatives."

"Some people are better at some things than you, but everybody has their own strengths and weaknesses."

"If ninety-five percent of the people are doing something, do something else, usually ninety-five percent of the people are wrong."

"Consider yourself lucky if you are able to get out of bed and go to work every day, and to carry out your normal biological functions. This is your miracle."

"If you have never had enough of anything, I can see why your behavior might be a little odd to some people."

"People who have been neglected, abused, and misused for most of their lives are going to have some obvious issues. They must work on developing their conscious level."

"If nobody tells you what's going on, and deliberately try to keep things from you, I guess you don't know what's going on."

"If you think your partner's behavior odd, what does that say about your behavior? Take a good look in the mirror."

"You may think your mate's behavior odd, but after being married fifty years, what does that say about you?"

"One of the reasons we have difficulties is because of what we think about ourselves."

"Why so much division, violence, hate, anger, and fear; what did I do to be so black and blue?"

"We've come a mighty long way, and we have a mighty long way to go."

"A lot of people didn't have a perfect background, but won't admit to it. None of our backgrounds are squeaky clean."

"Sometimes you think you are the only one you can trust, and frequently you may doubt if you can trust yourself."

"If you think nobody likes you, could it be that you don't like yourself?"

"There is always an alternative; don't give up."

"Failure is simply realizing that you need to re-evaluate your situation, and start again."

"We are all imprisoned by the facts of life."

"All of us are similar, just trying to find our
way through the sound and fury."

"If you are a child of ignorance, poverty, abuse,
neglect, and misuse; you must evaluate your situation,
develop your conscience level, and move forward.
Don't let your past determine your future."

"If you become self-destructive you are likely
to also become other-destructive."

"If you consistently make one deliberate step at a
time, you are likely to achieve your objectives."

"In life, we embark upon an incredible
journey. Some of us last longer and have
more advantages than others. But we all must
experience the many vicissitudes of life."

"The world is your oyster, relax and enjoy."

"Because of some of the past decisions you've
made, you will face some consequences
in your present and your future."

"Don't let other people tie knots in your life."

"Let go of things that don't develop or empower you."

"At some point you should cease to be the student and become the master teacher."

"In elementary logic, if your premise is false, anything added after that is untrue."

"If you don't see the facts and truths for yourself you do not have to believe."

"You won't get the most wonderful person in the world as your mate if you are carrying a lot of excess baggage."

"Nobody can read your mind; reveal to your love ones and significant others your most intimate hopes, wishes, and fears."

"Don't live your life by what somebody told you; figure out what you need to do for yourself."

"Don't set yourself up as the judge, jury, and executioner."

"It's not important what you can't do; it's only important what you can do."

"If you have never had enough of anything, don't feel like the lone stranger, you are in good company."

"Once you reach a certain age and level of maturity, you don't want to monkey around with making unnecessary changes in your life. It will destroy your total perspective and mind-set."

"When you experience poverty, neglect, abuse, and maltreatment; it's bound to be made manifest in your behavior."

"It's a big decision when you are faced with two forks in the road. But a general conclusion is that it is best to stick with the familiar, unless the familiar has become self- and other-destructive."

"It's easy to see what is apparent and obvious, but you must begin to see the complications behind it."

"If you begin your life in neglect, abuse, poverty, and maltreatment; you will be forever trying to improve your condition, even if you do some severe conscious development."

"If you start out behind the eight ball, don't try to make quantum leaps, take slow and incremental steps."

"Forget about what you didn't do yesterday, and focus on what you're going to do today."

"Sometimes we must say what needs to be said in order to get to where we want to go."

"One shouldn't fall in love; one should grow in love."

"You don't get married, you realize you are married, and that you both have become one."

"Love is not a feeling, it's something that you do. It's also a decision."

"Some people, who are in no better position than you, will tell you that you are not up to par. Don't let them deter you."

"Nobody can beat you at being yourself."

"If it's time to move on, give it up, don't hold on to a dream."

"If you have never had enough of anything, you tend to hoard whatever you get."

"Sometimes you have no alternative but to go along to get along."

"Sometimes we have been severely affected by something, and just are not aware of it; be sure you are aware of your own situation."

"If you think you have no more glory, think again, it' never too late to pursue your life-long goals."

"Don't get too hung up on outward appearances. You can dress a rhesus monkey and make it look adorable."

"Be aware that you need to get all the information, because you can't make a silk purse out of a sow's ear."

"If you come from an alcoholic, philandering, mentally ill, and otherwise multi-problem family; you are naturally going to have some issues in relating to the community and society."

"Don't let anyone convince you that you should be ashamed of your parents, yourself, or your community, you didn't create any of these things."

"If no one seems to want you around, and indicates that you need to leave town; remember, you have as much right to exist as anyone. Take control of your destiny."

"Nobody ever found fault with you over something you didn't say. Be selective in what you say."

"Your best intentions and efforts are sometimes misunderstood."

"A friend once told me that people have their own time-line for what they are going to do. Stopping them is like trying to stop a runaway locomotive."

"When you are isolated with little human
contact you learn a lot about yourself."

"If you have been berated, degraded, disrespected,
disregarded, overlooked, and underrated;
you are going to have some demons."

"Stop denying that you have issues
and demons to deal with."

"When you are comfortable with yourself
outside forces don't matter as much."

"When you can look up you can get up.
So, keep your eyes toward the sky."

"Once the ears hear something, and the brain
processes it, you can't disregard it."

"Don't waste time with people
trying to waste your time."

"Don't travel with people who don't
know where they're going."

"If we believe in the possibility of change, we
will do something to bring about change."

"Don't fight your brother, there are forces at work trying to destroy you and your brother, and are benefiting from your conflict."

"There's a difference between being a nuisance and being a threat."

"We should be on one accord, when we come together, there ain't nothing we can't do."

"Know when you became a man or woman and when you put away childish things."

"Don't be so preoccupied with yourself that you fail to see the suffering of other people."

"The paralysis of analysis: quit trying to analyze everything to the nth degree, just relax and take life as it comes."

"If your intuition tells you that something is bad for you, no matter how good it might seem, stay away from it, don't let it destroy you, thinking the problem might be in your judgment."

"What do you mean, that's just the way you are? Make some necessary changes in your life for the better."

"Adversity builds your strength; nobody ever achieved anything without overcoming some obstacles."

"Never go along to get along, if it doesn't somehow serve your purposes, don't get involved."

"If you can see no future for yourself, you need to correct you vision to 20/20."

"Be sure you are seeing things through unclouded lenses."

"Don't expect everybody to like you; everybody doesn't have your vision."

"We all have strengths and weaknesses; do what you do well to the fullest."

"If you don't love yourself you can't love anyone else."

"Everyone has the right to believe what they think is best for them."

"Don't try to change another person's reality."

"Don't try to change or get upset over what is happening in another person's life."

"Try to understand another person's pain even if you can't do anything about it."

"Don't condemn anyone as right or wrong, and always respect another person's choices."

"We should have nothing to say about what
another person does with their life."

"People usually make the best possible
choice they know to make at the time."

"Sometimes your best effort is not
good enough for some people."

"You can't make something more than it
is. Sometimes you have to admit, that's all
it is, and that's all it's going to be."

"Just when you think you've got it all
figured out, and getting ready to live, it's
time to depart from this world."

"You never do the things you wanted to do,
and the very things you said you wouldn't
do, you end up embracing. Such is life!"

"Most people manage to get through this life without
accomplishing what they wanted to accomplish."

"A good family, good schools, a decent church,
a resourceful community, and some good
basic institutions within that community, is
the best background one can have."

"All anyone can do is what they were trained to do."

"A lot of people will give their estimation of you, but it's difficult to estimate your motivation."

"Life is full of obstacles, but obstacles make us stronger."

"It's all right to party hardy, but be sure prior to the party, you take care of business."

"Don't overly frustrate yourself when you face a problem; you should always first consider your alternatives."

"If you keep getting up and showing up you will be ahead."

"Don't let other people convince you that you don't have a snowball's chance in hell. Only you can access your own motivation and determination."

"Without resources you will have little opportunities."

"We are in the position we're in mostly because of the choices we made, but some of our choices are made for us, and we can only follow through with the plan."

"Most people are queer to some degree. It's the nature of human beings."

"Your past is your past, forget it, and move on. Nobody's background is squeaky clean."

"People sometimes get comfortable in their insane condition, feeling this is normal."

"There will come a time when we will wish for a second chance, but such chances are rare, especially when history has moved on."

"Quit thinking about the past, you can't undo history, time is moving on."

"Sometimes life hands you a lemon, but you are still human and deserving of dignity and respect."

"There are no guarantees in this life on planet earth."

"You knew that situation was not healthy before you got into it; what do you mean what happened?"

"People have a history; they weren't born as they are, or as you presently see them."

"Being able to adjust is the key to our existence on this planet."

"In order to exist, people must make a wholesome adaptation to their environment, no matter how pathological the environment."

"Respect should be our birthright. We should have respect until we demonstrate that we don't deserve it, you shouldn't have to earn it."

"Everybody will have expectations of you, but you must follow your own dreams. Only you know the right way for you."

"Some things are too rich for our blood, as much as we hate to think so, but we should tread very carefully before we partake."

"You thought you had a rough time of it, but count your blessings, you pulled through it and survived."

"From what some of us have been through, it's a miracle we're still breathing."

"Be happy with your situation the way it is; don't worry about what your life could have been."

"Your enemy will often masquerade as your friend. Be sure you keep all of them in perspective."

"Be leery of people who smile in your face and plan deceit behind your back."

"Some people are like Chameleons, they can change on a dime, from positive to negative, be careful of them."

"Some people can smile at you while sticking a knife
in your jugular vein. They are raised that way."

"Don't let anyone cast you in the role of
victim; it is an undignified role."

"If you've got to hunt for food and water,
build a makeshift hut, and fight to survive
every day, you're not going to be concerned
with building a higher-level civilization."

"If you've got to plow the lower 40 acres
today, you won't be able to focus on
Crime and Punishment tonight."

"If you have mental health issues, philandering,
alcoholism, drug abuse, poverty, etc.,
in your background; naturally it's going
to affect the way you function."

"You knew your mate's background soon after you
met him or her; get over your righteous indignation."

"Some people will use, abuse, and misuse
you; and hate you for being the victim."

"Like Frankenstein, you created a monster, why
hate or try to destroy your own creation."

"If you're fortunate you will get it together before you pass away."

"The promised land is for everyone, but everyone will not get to the promised land."

CHAPTER 7

On Your Assignment

"Sure, some people are better off than you are,
but you have your own unique assignment."

"You have a God-given assignment; don't let
anyone keep you from your destiny."

"Sometimes your assignment is what you
decide it to be even though it is God-given."

"Some say you will never be happy until you are
engaged in carrying out your God-given assignment.
Whatever you and God has decided it to be."

"No matter what, all individuals have something
they are capable of doing at a high level,
but they must pursue perfecting it."

"Everybody can't be 'king-on-the-throne'; be what the Almighty God has called you to be."

"Nobody but you were designed to carry out your particular assignment in this given time, place, and space."

"Don't worry about other people; carry out your own assignment."

"If God had wanted somebody else, He wouldn't have made you. He made you for the purpose of carrying out a particular assignment in this place, space, and time."

"Carry out your assignment; you don't want to disappoint the Almighty God."

"Your assignment on this planet is what you and the Almighty God has decided it to be."

"The Almighty God never wanted you to be anything more than He or She intended you to be."

"Quit saying other people had better opportunities than you; you simply had a different assignment."

"Nobody can beat you at being you."

"Be sure you know what your assignment is, and try to develop it to the fullest extent."

"Of all things in life, it is most difficult
to figure out your assignment."

"Sometimes our background doesn't
prepare us to handle our assignment."

"Find your assignment and it will deliver you."

"Many people are unhappy because they fail to
engage in carrying out their assignment."

"Don't just find a job; try to find a job in
keeping with your assignment."

"You have a unique assignment; nobody can
handle your assignment better than you."

"When you are carrying out your assignment, you
are in your element, and you have few rivals."

"If you sometimes don't know what to do with yourself,
sit down and try to figure out what your assignment is."

"People will try to tell you that certain things are
not for you, but they don't know what's best for
you, and they don't know your assignment."

"Never quit until after you've had enough, become exhausted, or completed your assignment."

"Everybody has a God-given assignment, don't worry about other people, focus on your own assignment. Develop and work at mastering this assignment."

CHAPTER 8

On Education

"A fool can lose tomorrow looking back at yesterday;
but that same fool can lose yesterday, tomorrow,
and forever if he doesn't understand history."

"Your background and your education will
limit or propel you into the future."

"To many young people today don't like to read.
The slave master would be happy to know that after
all these years his conditioning is still strong."

"One can learn almost anything, if presented in a logical
order, and broken down into its basic components."

"If you think an education is a bad
thing to have try ignorance."

"Some children feel the less they work in school
the better off they are. They need guidance,
encouragement, and a firm hand."

"You have only two options: improve your
educational level, or live a substandard existence."

"The minute you recognize that your educational
achievement is directly proportional to your own efforts
you will begin to improve your overall situation."

"Everyone's knowledge is finite; don't believe
you know more than you know."

"If your knowledge of Black history is limited to slavery,
then you know very little about Black history."

"There's a difference between knowledge and
wisdom: knowledge is having information, being
able to apply that information is wisdom."

"The powers that be are happy, just as the
slave master was pleased, if we were slow to
pick up a book and read. They want to see you
ignorant. Get all the education you can."

"If your parents were inadequate, it
doesn't speak well for your future, without
a lot of conscious development."

"If teachers don't like you, maybe you have some issues you need to deal with. Teachers are human too, but they usually are equality oriented."

"We are programed on a daily basis to behave in a negative manner."

"A good education is the most important thing you can attain in this technological, democratic, and capitalistic society."

"Without proper training from a good family, schools, community, church, and other institutions; you are likely to become pathological in your behavior, and a burden to the community and the society."

"If you don't get a good education, you will forever have difficulty negotiating the social, economic, and political systems."

"We must be properly trained and educated in order to function well in a modern capitalistic, technological, and democratic society."

"For some people an education is a new concept."

"Some things are natural: birds fly, snakes crawl, and eagles soar. They don't have to be taught."

"I heard a Black person say once that they hadn't read a book since high school. The slave master would be proud of them."

"Most people would do better if they knew better; the problem with most people is they don't know any better."

"A good education is basic, without this education, you will be lost in a world of dung."

"We can't just 'let the hair go with the hide': we must educate, care for, cultivate, and train our children."

"If your education was inadequate, you will be forever behind the eight ball, until you decide to do something about it."

"If you had to learn everything by trial and error, you received a lot of bumps and bruises."

"If you don't know how much you don't know, keep making an effort, you can overcome."

"If nobody ever taught you much of anything, then I guess you don't know much of anything."

"An education should bring out what is already within you, rather than teach you to memorize a lot of useless information."

"If a teacher only says something the student already knows, the teacher is wasting the student's time."

CHAPTER 9

On Success

"Keep your mind on success and success on your mind."

"The only reason why you failed is
because you weren't prepared."

"So, you didn't apply yourself at the
beginning, it's never too late. Get going."

"Sometimes the least likely to succeed becomes
the most successful. And the one who labeled him
or her as such becomes the least successful."

"Most people quit because of fear
they will fail. Keep at it!"

"If you didn't come from a perfect background,
you can still achieve you dreams."

"Nobody ever achieved their dreams
without getting help from others, even if
you are not aware of who they were."

"If you can go to good schools, attend a good
church, and locate in a good community; you can
likely thrive in your environment. These things are
not panaceas but will get you off to a good start."

"The answer to the successful resolution of your
problems lie in your subconscious mind."

"Some people advance themselves better
because they have better and more favorable
social, economic, political, psychological, and
educational factors in their background."

"What you achieve in life mainly depends on the choices
you make, not on circumstances or happenstance."

"The only way to read that 700-page book, without
feeling a strain, is to read it one page at a time."

"The only way to write a book is to write one
page, one chapter, one section at a time."

"If everyone you know implies that you can't succeed,
you can still make it if you continue to work diligently."

"People will tell you that your game is lame,
and that you have no rightful claim, but you
can still be successful in the game."

"It is the right person, that is in the right
place, that comes along at the right time,
that ends up making history."

"Consistently work at developing your weaknesses, and
fortifying your strengths, if you want to be a success."

"If you don't see yourself as a success,
you probably won't be a success."

"You can do everything necessary for your
development, but in the end, you must
know how to work the system."

"Success in life depends on having
made a supreme effort."

"If your great-grandparents were once
sharecroppers, and you feel you have no future,
think again. With a little determination you
can achieve some degree of success."

"Success is the best form of revenge."

"Success in life mainly depends upon your family background, your educational background, the luck-of-the-draw, and the amount of effort you put forth."

CHAPTER 10

On Attitude

"Jealousy and envy can bring us to a
self- and other-destructive level."

"No matter what, keep a positive attitude."

"Don't ever let your future become a minor concern."

"Things may seem bad, but regardless of the
circumstances, stay focused, and keep being positive."

"Get clarity, get focused, and keep moving forward."

"The only thing keeping you from climbing
that mountain is the doubt in your mind."

"Keep you mind on integrity and
integrity on your mind."

"The only reason why a butterfly can fly is
because nobody ever told it that it couldn't."

"Give people the benefit of the doubt, but you
must always be concerned about yourself."

"The only sure way of achieving your
objectives is to take it one step at a time."

"Nobody ever achieved their objectives
by being rude or obnoxious."

"If you don't believe you can you probably won't."

"If you lie, you'll cheat; if you cheat, you'll steal;
and if you steal, you'll commit murder."

"It's a thin line between love and hate."

"You can't save a person unless they want to be saved."

"Make time to help your brother or sister."

"Some journeys we must make alone."

CHAPTER 11

On Family

"Be respectful to all others, to yourself,
and especially to your family."

"Your home should be the most
sacred place on the planet."

"Always support your family; emotionally,
physically; and provide them with unconditional
love, attention, and affection."

"In raising our children, sometimes we are not
functioning from a skill-set, we are only treating
our children the way we were treated."

"If your parents didn't relate to you, you will have
difficulty relating to your children. Try not to pass it on."

"Sacrifice your life, your body, and
your brain for you family."

"If necessary, fall on a sword, to protect your family."

"There is no one way to be a man for your
family. You've got to figure out for yourself
what is a good definition of manhood."

"Family love should be the strongest possible love."

"Regardless of what you want for your children
they are going to find their own way."

"If parents don't like you, it can only be
yours or your parents' problem."

"Be generous to all, but take care of family
first, charity begins at home."

"Say your father left you before you were
born, the slave master would be happy that his
conditioning has lasted all these years."

"We must understand our historical conditioning and
how it has contributed to our family problems."

"Love and respect your family, but if you can't
get along with them, treat them like everyone
else—leave them to boil in their own oil."

"The measure of a man is how he relates to his family."

"If your family doesn't think enough of you to
confront you, and tell you what they are thinking,
you need to re-evaluate your situation."

"Even if your family rejects your love, you should
still love them, for as long as they will let you."

"Even if your love ones don't return your love,
you should love them unconditionally."

"Don't love your family to get love in return;
you love them only to give of yourself."

"You should have a love for your family beyond
comprehension. But don't negate common
sense, or give up your self-respect."

"Family love is a constant journey
to provide what they need."

"Family love is forgiving; knowing that
one's intentions were good."

"A devoted family man will find it hard to
walk away. He will almost destroy himself
before abandoning his family."

"Sometimes one parent will degrade the other parent in front of the children. This does more to destroy the children themselves and the whole family than any other single factor."

"Even though your children act as though they hate you, always give them unconditional love."

"Try to create a pleasant atmosphere in your family: emotionally and physically."

"A disrespectful, neglectful, and abusive parent doesn't deserve any respect."

"If you seriously do the best you can for your family, what else can anyone expect? But be sure you have exhausted your efforts."

"Be more concerned about what your family relationship is like at home, rather than its appearance in public."

"No matter what happens, be able to say, I did the best I could for my family, regardless of how the situation turned out."

"Material things are good for your children, we live in materialistic society, but don't just throw these material things at them. Be sure you take time to establish a relationship with them."

"Be sure you don't infantilize your children. They must grow up and become independent. By doing this you destroy their potential futures."

"If you don't invest in your children emotionally and financially, don't expect a significant return."

"Even your mother, father, brother, husband, children, sister, wife, and relatives will cross you. Be sure you are flexible enough to withstand the tide."

"Don't give up on your family unless there is no other way; always keep hope alive."

"Nothing should give a man more pleasure than to see his family loving, living, playing, working, and otherwise enjoying life."

"A man should not pass away without being able to say that he was a good provider for his family."

"If it took you fifty years to see that you had made a poor choice for your mate, what does that say for you?"

"When people finally go their separate ways, one of them probably had a time-line for how long it was going to last."

"It takes two to cement a relationship. When the relationship fails usually both parties

are to blame. Though, one of them will
often put the blame on the other."

"Parents are the child's role model; children
will be much like their parents, unless they
work on developing their conscious level."

"When you are younger you see your parents
as all-knowing; as you get older you begin
to doubt their wisdom; but as you mature
you begin to highly value their advice."

"If one does not come from a unified family,
he or she will have no basis for any type of
unification with anyone or anything."

"Children need direction and guidance, if
parents and teachers don't train them, how are
they supposed to know how to behave."

"If your parents were disfranchised, and their parents
were disfranchised, chances are you will start out
behind the eight ball, and will have to play catch up."

"Without conscious development, a son
is likely to be much like his father, and
daughter much like her mother."

"The American dream is for the children
to do better than their parents."

"If your parents and grandparents didn't leave you an inheritance, don't fret, God bless the child that's got his own."

"The family that commiserates together builds strong relationships and will likely stay together."

CHAPTER 12

On Relationships

"Get attached to people based on their character, attitude, and behavior, rather than their race or ethnicity."

"You should have known when you saw your partner acting a fool that they were carrying some excess baggage."

"Some people begin a relationship with no intentions of it lasting. They have already picked a time and place for it to end."

"Don't go into a relationship feeling the person can make you happy."

"To stay and repair a relationship and stay sane takes effort; especially when one party has decided it is time to depart."

"Don't try to hold on to a relationship that is completely dead, and in fact was dead on arrival."

"No matter how much you want your relationship to last, if it is over, let it go."

"If your relationship was over before it got started, realize that fact, and bring it to a close."

"Some relationships were begun under false pretense, and were not meant to last."

"Sometimes one party in a relationship decides that it is time for it to end, for one reason or the other, don't demean yourself by trying to hold on."

"A couple will often decide that one of them has to be out of town by sundown, and the town isn't big enough for the two of them."

"Sometimes people bring too much baggage to a relationship for it to last very long."

"Take time to know the other party before getting involved in a relationship."

"You can't make another person love
you if the feeling is gone."

"Sometimes in a relationship there was
never any love to begin with."

"People get into a relationship for different
reasons: sometimes the reasons are
more negative than positive."

"In some relationships, one party will decide, the
only option is to try and destroy the other party."

"Some relationships are established
for destructive purposes."

"In some relationships, from the beginning,
you are being set up for the slaughter."

"Sometimes you make every possible effort, and
the relationship still doesn't work, even after many
years, know when it's time to walk away."

"Come on! you could read the signs; you knew
your relationship was headed for destruction."

"Some people are too self- and other-destructive
to be involved in a good-positive relationship."

"Some people bring too much destructive baggage to a relationship for it to last. In that case it's just a matter of time."

"Some people go into a relationship not expecting it to last. In that case it probably won't."

"Some people do everything they can to assure that their relationship won't last."

"Trust your spirit, if you spirit tells you that a relationship is not going to work, make an agreeable departure."

"People go into a relationship for a reason, a season, or a lifetime; at some point get the necessary clarification as to why you are in your relationship."

"Don't get angry because your destructive plans for your relationship didn't work out like you thought."

"As you get older, sometimes your mate will want to trade you in on a younger model."

"Everybody brings some baggage to a relationship."

"Acknowledge that you brought baggage to your relationship, and try to get beyond it by improving your conscious level."

"When your best isn't good enough in a relationship, you have to either try harder or move on."

"Some people are not meant to stay in your life forever, only to connect for a short while, and plant some important seeds."

"When a person has many negative behaviors don't go into a relationship expecting to change them."

"Don't get upset over the person's behavior; you chose to get into that negative relationship."

"Let the spirit lead you in walking away from a relationship, but be sure you're not dead by the time you make the decision to walk away."

"If you know in your spirit a relationship is not going to work, give it up."

"When your partner wants to trade you in on a newer model, be happy for them, but don't sacrifice yourself."

"Don't be so quick to form a relationship; be sure you have all the necessary information about the other individual."

"No matter how hard you try in a relationship sometimes you can't save it. People have their own agendas; and are sometimes sporadic, erratic, and unpredictable."

"Life is raunchy, if people in a relationship fail to make an effort, life is going to be tough."

"When you have a relationship with someone who is self- and other-destructive, it can be a challenge trying to survive."

CHAPTER 13

On Miscellaneous

"Stay away from inappropriate things, they may not be against the law, but will still get you into trouble."

"Make a decision and intend to follow through on everything you do, even if you do sometimes fall short of the mark."

"Let your life be about more than drinking, philandering, gambling, expensive cars, and fine clothes. Material things are especially fleeting at best."

"Be careful in labeling people. We are all sad, weak, sorry, and pitiful at times. These are relative terms. It depends on who and what context you refer."

"If you don't tell people what you are thinking,
how do you expect them to be aware of the
dynamics of your behavior and actions."

"Do the best you can for everyone concerned;
it will all come out in the wash."

"Everyone should take a brick to the monument,
for building culture, institutions, and civilization."

"Everybody is an immigrant; be respectful of those
who come to this country many years later."

"Don't get too caught up on someone else's style,
because it will always change in a while."

"Human behavior is not complex, it just
seems that way, usually our behavior is based
on our training and conditioning."

"Psychological problems are directly proportional
to the amount of stress over a period of time."

"Social, political, economic, psychological,
and educational forces sometimes conspire
to do like gravity—pull us down."

"Sometimes people need a scapegoat to cast
their anger, fear, frustration, and hostility upon.
It makes them feel better about themselves."

"People engage in a lot of random-meaningless communication; it's up to you to decide what has validity."

"We don't know how long anyone is going to be in our lives. Love them when they come, and love them when they go."

"If you are an adult, don't get caught up in playing childish games."

"If there was no love, care, affection, or attention in your home; you are likely to get behind the eight ball, but you can survive if you work at developing your conscious level."

"If you can't get along, why get it on?"

"So, what if you think nobody likes you, be good to yourself."

"The man who hasn't made any enemies hasn't achieved anything."

"People may disrespect you and say you don't have it all together, but keep getting up and keep moving, you will be far ahead in the game."

"We have been socialized to believe a man has to be aggressive, violent, competitive, hyper-masculine, a warrior, and a fighter; but you must arrive at your own definition of manhood."

"Never judge a man by his achievements, but how far he has come to make those achievements."

"If you had better opportunities, you could have been a contender."

"If you can't manage your responsibilities someone else will."

"Quit thinking that business idea you had is a good idea for somebody else, develop and use it yourself."

"You don't have to tell an eagle how to soar, how to hunt its prey, or how to build its nest. It just comes natural."

"Don't take out your righteous indignation on your community. Learn to contribute rather than be destructive."

"At some point all of us will come to a crisis in our lives, and it will be necessary to make a change."

"Most people are afraid of change, but change is the only constant."

"The only way to grow, develop, and get to where
you want to go, is to experience vulnerability."

"Most people are afraid to try new things
because they are afraid of failure."

"Don't become so overwhelmed with your situation
that you can't see the forest for the trees."

"You may feel like an orphan who have never had
enough of anything, but you must have—you survived."

"A higher level of technology does not
mean a higher level of civilization."

"Liberating people is not a popular
vocation or avocation."

"If we all work together, we can
solve the world's problems."

"Everyone won't cooperate, but make an
effort to bring out the best in people."

"Be careful of the man who writes his own references."

"Being a leader can sometimes be difficult:
there are always those who think you are right,
and those who think you are wrong."

"Defend someone's honor only if they conduct themselves in an honorable way toward you."

"It's easy to reminisce about the past, but what are you going to do today."

"Do a good job the first time, and the customer will always seek out your services."

"It's always the behind the scene individuals that are the backbone of the organization."

"Social scientists say, 'we are born into the world a blank slate'; after that, because of inadequate parents, and a poor environmental situation, some of us tend to regress rather than move forward in a normal fashion."

"When you really have something valuable, you have something most people don't have."

"The solution will not be found in the final solution."

"Some people take a job in a profession where they could possibly have some hang ups or conflicts. They feel they can resolve their conflicts by being in proximity with certain people. It is the worst possible reason for going into a profession."

"When your role model is pathological you need to be careful in your identification."

"Be able to tell if a person is limited,
challenged, or simply lacks exposure."

"Most geniuses have some difficulties with social
relationships, but there are exceptions to all rules."

"That girl or boy is beautiful, and you would
like to get to know them, but before you do,
be sure and take that second look."

"It's highly important for some people to fit in, and
they will do just about anything to be accepted."

"The latest and most expensive car, the biggest house,
and the finest clothes are good to have. But don't
sell your soul to the devil to obtain these things."

"The greatest single quality one
can have is adaptability."

"When you find yourself in conflict, and
everyone is acting like a child; remember,
someone has to be an adult."

"Don't just run in place while going nowhere."

"When you meet new people, get to know their
background, before you get involved with them."

"Never interrupt your enemy while he
is busy destroying himself."

"Don't think you got away with something.
One twinkling of an eye, and your whole
world can come tumbling down."

"Never argue about something when you
know you don't have all the information."

"Money always flows through our hands. It's
not what you make it's what you keep."

"If you have no facts or evidence,
you have no argument."

"Get your own self together first, then spend
time trying to help other people."

"When the truth is told, it's difficult not to respond
to it, even if you don't want to respond."

"Can't we all just get along? When you
respect me as a man, we can get along."

"Now that you are awake, what's your next move?"

"People with good hearts must be careful who
they listen to and let influence them."

"A lot of people project what they feel about themselves onto other people."

"Before you start telling people how to live their lives, ask yourself, who asked you?"

"Don't live in the past; times have changed."

"Be kind, considerate, and understanding of all those whom you encounter."

"Don't beat yourself up because you missed a few opportunities in your life; everybody has missed a few opportunities."

"You only thought that particular thing was desirable, and you couldn't do without it, you let your imagination run wild."

"Quit making excuses, do the best you can with what you've got, and shut the hell up!"

"If you expect to find life a rose garden, you better look on another planet."

"Quit putting off today for tomorrow, the time is here, right now."

"Any job is an improvement over no job at all."

"Some people have a snowball's chance in hell of making it through a neglectful and abusive family, a deteriorated community, inadequate schools, and an otherwise dreadful life."

"It is common for many young people to demonstrate immaturity and poor judgment. It is rare for teenagers to have a well-developed sense of conscience. At a young age all they know is mostly what you teach them."

"The truth to some people is only propaganda to others."

"Sometimes people see you as incorrigible, and going to hell in a hand basket, but you can turn that around."

"Allow others the freedom to be themselves."

"When we are young, we are sometimes impulsive and immature, but we must grow up, forget our childhood, and move on with our lives."

"Don't continue to hold an impulsive, mischievous, and immature childhood against a reformed adult. People do change."

"What you see is only a part of what you get."

"We always have the strongest desire for
something we haven't been exposed to."

"The key to a healthy life is learning to
respect the boundaries of other people."

"What's appropriate in one place could
be inappropriate in another."

"Be the first to offer congratulations, and
the last to engage in degradation."

"Read between the lines, don't just see what's
apparent, you knew that wasn't going to work."

"You can play a person for a while, but you can't play on
them forever. Even a fool will get wise—eventually."

"On many occasions those you love will betray you,
but you are a hustler, get back in the game."

"Be leery of people who bites the
hand that feeds them."

"The person who sabotages the one that's
trying their best to provide for him or her is
carrying some excess baggage. One needs to
distance themselves from such a person."

"If you say you already know what I'm telling you, then why do you act the way you do?"

"If you listen to an idiot's advice and follows it, then you cannot be trusted."

"When you are grasping for straws you may not be careful who you listen to. Sometimes you will listen to anyone offering advice."

"Struggle, competition, adversity, and obstacles are what drives the nation. They keep us all in an alert frame of mine."

"Nothing but a moron would marry someone with the specific intent to destroy them."

"Lack of exposure to something can cause it to seem like a pleasant alternative to what you have access to."

"Don't confuse the messenger with the message or the dancer with the dance."

"When you realize you did the best you could for what you knew at the time, at some point you have to let it go."

"Coal under years of extreme pressure turns into diamonds; you are a diamond in the rough."

"If someone does something good for you
they deserve something good in return."

"Friends come in many colors."

"Go to the limit for your friends, but
not at your own expense."

"If your so-called friends don't support you,
you need to find some new friends."

"A true friend would never turn his back
on you or let you down, triangulate you, or
encourage you into unwholesome activity."

"If you are self-destructive you are
likely to be other-destructive."

"If you come from a lower-level background,
people will encourage you to function at that
level—due to environmental inertia."

"Don't let your environment determine
your destiny: be in it, but not of it."

"Be careful of the vibrations you give off
for they will return to you triple-fold."

"Just because people are not shooting cannons
at you it doesn't mean you are not in a war."

"The powers that be believes the masses
are stupid and behave like sheep."

"Don't label another person as stupid or
ignorant: sometimes our behavior is strange
because we are in a desperate struggle to
survive, adapt, adjust, and change."

Printed in the United States
By Bookmasters